Danbury Library, Danbury, CT
danburylibrary.org

 **W9-AVD-109**

# Adventures in Cartooning

James Sturm
Andrew Arnold
Alexis Frederick-Frost

:01
First Second
New York & London

For Eva and Charlotte
-JS

For Mom and Dad
-AA

For Grandma, Leslie, Mom and Dad
-AFF

# Once upon a time... a princess tried to make a comic...

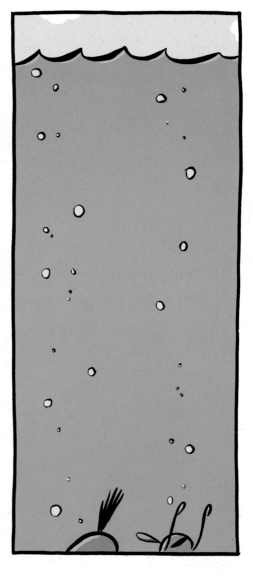

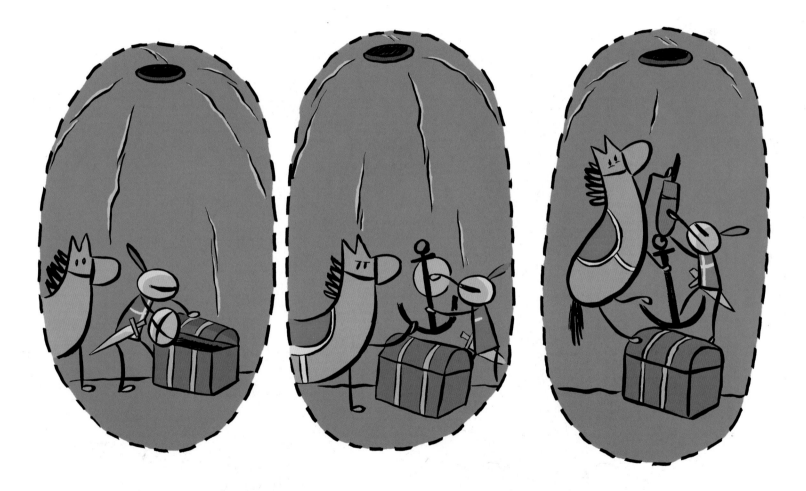

!
Over here!
HELP!
Save us!
We t
Help us!
Turned into
Tried to steal
We were knigh
Unbelievable! Talking vegetables!
We raided the dragon's ca
Turned into vegetables
There is only
We got caught
HELP US!
We were knights

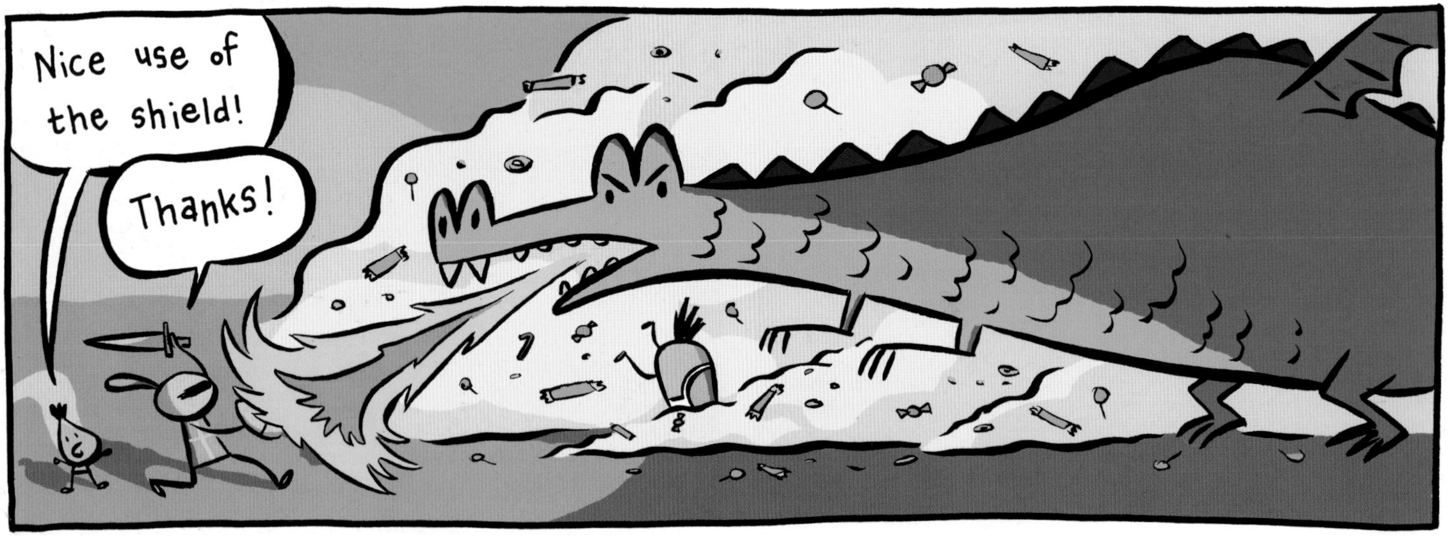
Nice use of the shield!
Thanks!

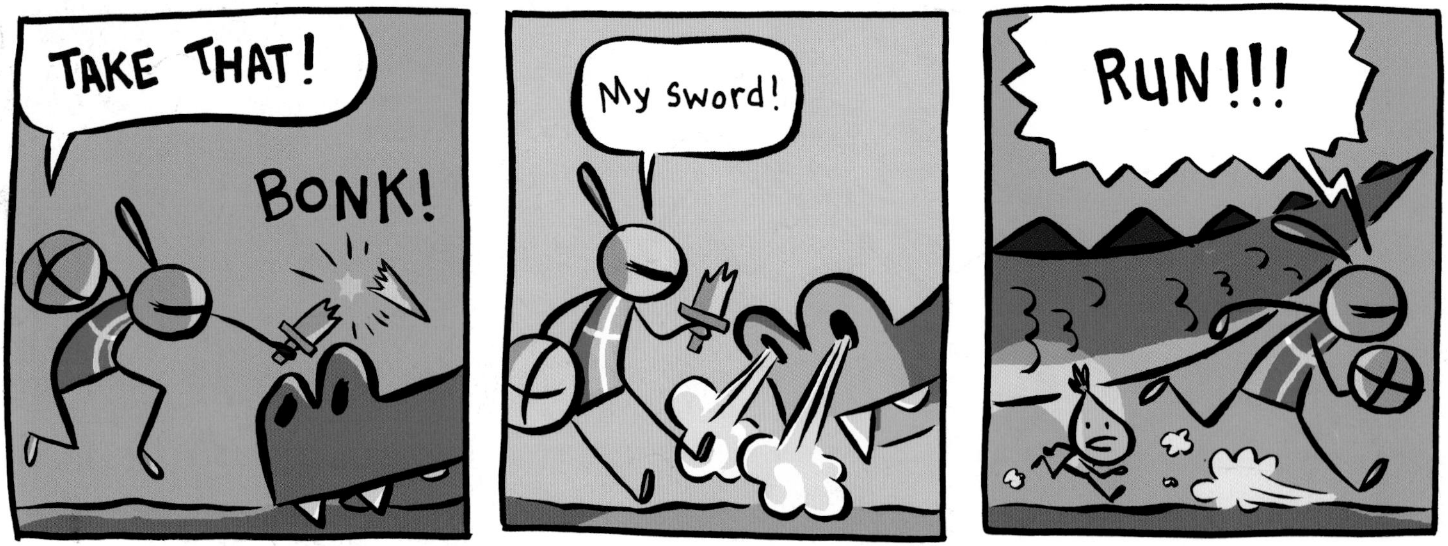
TAKE THAT!
BONK!
My sword!
RUN!!!

BACK TO THE VEGETABLES!
Once we change them back to knights, there will be enough of us to beat the dragon!
Unless he eats us first!

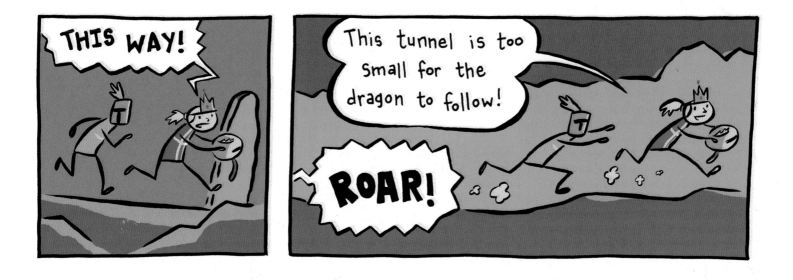

THE END

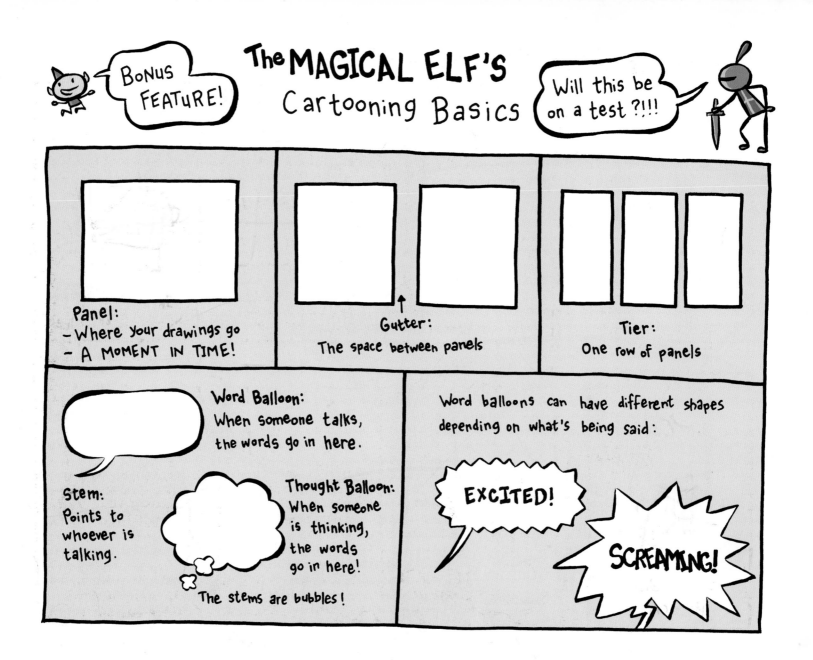

The MAGICAL ELF'S Cartooning Basics

BONUS FEATURE!

Will this be on a test?!!!

**Panel:**
- Where your drawings go
- A MOMENT IN TIME!

**Gutter:**
The space between panels

**Tier:**
One row of panels

**Word Balloon:**
When someone talks, the words go in here.

**Stem:**
Points to whoever is talking.

**Thought Balloon:**
When someone is thinking, the words go in here!

The stems are bubbles!

Word balloons can have different shapes depending on what's being said:

EXCITED!

SCREAMING!

This book grew out of an assignment given by James Sturm at the Center for Cartoon Studies in White River Junction, VT using Ed Emberly's book, **Make a World**, as inspiration. Alexis Frederick-Frost and Andrew Arnold were students in the school's very first class! Thanks, Ed Emberly!

For more information on the Center for Cartoon Studies, visit www.cartoonstudies.org

The knight

Edward

Elf

I see you!

Ok! Now YOU try drawing a story! Grab some paper and a pencil or pen!!!
Here's a great example of how to do it!
A Fishy Story
BY Eva
Move
I-I cant
Splash
Help

First Second

New York & London

Copyright © 2009 by James Sturm,
Andrew Arnold & Alexis Frederick-Frost

Published by First Second
First Second is an imprint of Roaring Brook Press, a division of
   Holtzbrinck Publishing Holdings Limited Partnership
175 Fifth Avenue, New York, NY 10010

All rights reserved

Distributed in the United Kingdom by Macmillan Children's Books,
   a division of Pan Macmillan.

Cataloging-in-Publication Data is on file at the Library of Congress
ISBN: 978-1-59643-369-4

First Second Books are available for special promotions and premiums.
For details, contact: Director of Special Markets, Holtzbrinck Publishers.

First Edition April 2009
Printed in March 2011 by South China Printing Co. Ltd.,
Dongguan City, Guangdong Province

10 9 8 7

BY ART WE LIVE